P9-AGN-879

Nancy Sullivan

TELLING IT

DAVID R. GODINE

BOSTON

David R. Godine, Publisher
Boston, Masschusetts

Copyright © 1965, 1966, 1969, 1971, 1972, 1973, 1974, 1975
by Nancy Sullivan

LCC 74-30909
ISBN 0-87923-121-1
Printed in the United States of America

Acknowledgments: some of these poems first appear-
ed in: *Body English, Hellcoal Press, Choice, The Massa-
chusetts Review, The Nation, The New Republic, Poetry
Bag, Quarterly Review of Literature, Southern Review, Vir-
ginia Quarterly Review*. 'To My Body' was first
published in *Poetry*.

A Godine Poetry Chapbook
Second Series

LIBRARY
University of Texas
At San Antonio

Telling It

Life Suite

1. she views her birth

She imagines what went before
to determine the birth she shall celebrate.
How she came into herself.
She wonders if there was pleasure
one night, possibly two when
the display started in the scattering of gold

and continued until the rolled-up person
uncoiled into girl.
Her veins decorated her with a design more Persian
than on a rug from there.
In the curved comfort of the womb,
the tight little face could focus on nothing.
The fists pounded the liquid, exploring
who knows for what, or even how that motion was.
Then out.
Born they say . . .
But that night of beginning was the becoming.
Only the trees shifting colors from season to season
tell her anything now of that spectacular time
in the womb when she made no mistakes.
The birth ended the bobbing and floating.
Now only those thrust into space in barbarous suits
can know how it was before she left.

2. her education

Sounds in the morning rise like steam,
the hissing of daily noises
sputtering the gravest lesson: every day
the same day, give or take a sound.
So parades the great education.

She is fourteen.
The brightness of each day dulls long before the sun.
Through the window she sees the same grass grow
        over and over.

Foul armies crowd the history books.
Logarithms and triangles clash on a march to the answer.
Rushed to the school where thick rulers govern
and holy beads chain the way out,
she in a middy returns her carriage
to type: 'Alfie was a good boy
and his brother better.' Now again, girls.
Dailiness.
Repeat the great lesson:
On, on, on.
She is twenty
and the years rattle.
Same grass, same flowering tree—
over and over practicing leaf-making.

3. she loves

The deep days widened.
    A chorale of voices in her skin
        called him to her.

Love came in sounds
    like the rush of horses.
        She rode it wildly.

Nothing changed position,
    but she moved to meet it
        through shifting tenses.

She tread his promises
    as on buoyant water
        spoiling at its spring.

He left like rocks
    in the blare of morning.
        She hums the chorus.

4. she marries

Not the Indian Chief,
not that exotic man the playful buttons
had always promised.

She chose the lawyer from a polished firm,
who like a surgeon cut through her flesh
toward bone into the scrabble of her
to sever in the law and make her his.

Into his moderate income house she moved
avoiding the thick leather of his legal library
filled to the binding with precedents.

She married marriage.

The bed was a convent of a private order
where, its abbess, she dispenses swift consecrations.

She boiled up sensuous stews.
She renewed the living room. The lawyer's path
was decorated until his heart ran out.

With all the buttons dangling, she wed again,
a garrulous Armenian who knew deep secrets
about the heavy duet of man and woman.
Almost happy, she lived it through.

5. *her child*

At first he was blond, briefly gold,
with hair like the edges of the sun.
Then, as at an eclipse, he darkened
and became all the shadowy men
of her dreaming.

He was better than the theory of him.
All she knew of the nights that had
made him became now a crowd
of love in her eyes to accompany him
to his betrayal.

He grew in bounty for her possession.
His legs grew long to hasten him
out of the nursery into puberty.
Loving and guileless as a lover,
she confused him.

What the Army drafted was a boy no longer.
In the swift suit of war, a wanton
Private, he loved without her. In rich disguises
he wrote her letters.

6. she waits

Observing the outside of everything
now when not to front life is her lot,
she measures steps
to a store grinning in discounts,
to a movie where others also sit
alone in the plush to watch the perfect people
stretched giant on the giant screen
speak over not to them in the dialogue
of a woven life. The audience turns,
always away, to disperse toward empty
places. Walking behind the lonely shoulders,
she sees in sudden sculpture the still essential
contour of their fat time gone down.

7. her death

Despite, it came.
Like an active worm, intestines all in a knot.

Possibly at sea, everyone shocked,
'She's not old, only in the middle of a life
still filled with promise.'
Stitched into an envelope,
canvas and rope, by seamen
given to different tailoring.
Dropped. Into a wave.

Possibly in a bed, a tangle of tubes
dangling. Everything hushed
and flat, a priest mumbling.
Flowers for a funeral already there.

Straining the worn pulleys, the modish box
drops. Into Schenectady.

Possibly by bomb. All and one.
A mammoth bed to huddle on.
Then in a hush of ashes the bodies
turn into statues, artifacts
as at Pompeii and after Vesuvius.
Dropped. Into history.
This man finishing a sentence,
that one turning a key. She frying an egg.
Dying all the while when, in a sudden flash, she did.

To My Body

I am in the tub with my body.
I look down at it from inside my face.

'Body,' I say, 'you're a foreign person.
We've been together all this time
and still, in very serious ways,
we are strangers.'

The body smiles on the water.

'You're not all lean and bone
as you are in my head.
You bulge in the tub.
There are bubbles clinging
to this wedge of curling moss.
These breasts are cantaloupe.
I don't understand, given the chance,
how you could reproduce,
how you could get me out of yourself
to make room for another.
(There are many problems we'd have to work out.)
In a sense, you've had me,
and I'm glad I have you.
We're enough trouble to each other.'

Six Kisses

after Rodin's *The Kiss*

I

No longer itself
the hand on that bare thigh
becomes the woman it touches.
The two merge in the hush.
Their skin sweats through the stone.

2

She brings news to the blood,
promises to the mouth.
Their ruly hairs combine.
For once, nothing is wrong.

3

The parts in touching kiss
and in parting touch on what it is
a kiss is.

4

Who speaks? No one.
The tongue, ripe as a noun,
tastes of poems.

5

The arch of arm, the foot's arch.
Every nerve confides in another.
The mouth was made for such involvement.
This kiss causes them wonder, causes them
panic, joy.

6

They are each other.

Menu Poems

1. rare meat

That's what we are.
We are rare meat spring fed
on the blood's broth.
Chuck and clod, the liver and lights
pulse in that market under the skin
across from the pilot heart.

I order the tender loin
for the rare meal rarely done
but end up with a clod
covered with sauces.
It's not what I wanted.
Butcher, you deceive me
as you cut me apart.

2. backbone

The whittled rings
no longer taper to tail.
Backbone.
Who willed me the strength
to stand up as well as back?
I know how position tempts me,
how the prime cuts challenge my blade.
Everything bubbles on simmer.
My stew is confused
with rosemary, memory's herb.

Comfort me, creatures in jars
preserved for viewing, for remembering.
I've meals to make and the clock has turned back
to where there's no going.
Backbone.

The recipe is old and it's blurring.
I've no use for the long menu,
no use for concocting talented pies.
The absolute meal is of flesh, blood, and bone
as the gods knew who consumed it
        as they were consumed.
The backbone narrows and brings me back
to where the stew bubbles
in me, on the body's range.

I Want an X-Ray of You

What I need is to gather some assurance
that inside you our structures coincide.
What I need is to invade your flesh completely.
I want an X-ray of you.
The camera contacts a flat world flatly
and no one paints the outside outside anymore.
Edge, side, down, round,
end, up, bottom, top,
beneath, roof, cellar, whatever;
fence, field: the areas we measure.
I need an X-ray of you.

Head

First an X-ray of your brain
with all its separate televisions blasting
underneath the cranium's fantastic music shell.
Your brain's all theatre, even here,
my entertaining lover.
In this city that was once your face
I trace the rugged masonry of mouth
and your eyes, the canyons of your eyes.
When I touch your hair, what in there tingles?
When I lick your ear, who sends the telegram?
In the grey-white shadows of the cerebellum
I recognize the softness that surrounds you
but know the hard bone clarifies.
It's the calcium that wears.

Chest

Your heart's caged in
inside a pirate's chest.
I hope to find me in there,
grinning like a donut
in some awful album photo,
a positive within this negative of you.
No? Then the ouija camera flubbed
and I may return this proof.
The heart's a hollow organ, invisible
when no one's in it.

Pelvis

How perfect this empty basin
empty of fruit, perfectly empty.
It spreads to a curve just slightly
different from me.
No curling hairs, no significant
signs of your sex or mine.

We are Adam and Eve,
Hansels or Gretels,
the shadows are fig leaves
fading, receding inside.

I recognize your pelvis, false and true.
I recognize your pelvic arch. This is a good likeness
because when I knew your hardness
I knew it in the dark.

Hand

You always said your hands were ugly
but see how really like rare whittled stone,
this left one pointing upward
all the knuckles knocking,
the joints raided and doric.
I sampled these bones
through their gloves of flesh,
each digit and metacarpus,
held so often in my own.
But to see them in this luminous X-ray
is to separate them from that pattern.
I touch their spare design to celebrate
the hand within your hand.

Foot

You would never think I'd want
an X-ray of your foot. I do.
I want to learn those feet
that brought you to me
to understand them better
when you don't come back.
Tarsus and metatarsus,
that ankle bone like a pauper's hill
and all the rippled toes
that poked pyramids in the sheets
we've tangled under.

Look! Would you think that these
frail devices could carry you,
all your bones above, gristle,
muscle, tissue, flesh?
From this brave pedestal
your entire scaffold rises.
I see in them the end and start again.

Two Orgasms

1

More like the candle going out
with the smoke still stroking the air,
more like that than the sudden blackness
after the lightning.

2

At Lascaux they've shut the caves
because the dampness is ruining
the running beasts on the slippery walls.
Only the experts enter to grope
through the moist, spectacular
canal. Once there, someone raises
a torch. The walls blaze
and for a moment
the world's just been discovered.

The World Is Surfaces

We are on it not in it,
    the world I mean.
A photograph taken from the moon
    shows the land as beaches
covering the sphere
    in erratic blankets
with sprawling bathers on them.

On walks on top of the land
    I learn it's true.
And no matter how long I wear it,
    my skin, a constant
surprise, keeps me all together
    when my insides collide.
I don't believe in the core,

or in getting down to essentials.
    I don't believe in the marrow
but in the bone outside, the gun's barrel.
    The painting's surface is it.
As my hand strokes this suede coat
    to soothe the chafed skin
of the animal it covered

as it now covers me in my cover,
    I want the shell of a tortoise,
the gross dome of the mosque,
    the crust of Alaska,
and every membrane over the inner places
    everywhere, everywhere.
The world is surfaces.

21

Cripples at the Dance

Braced, crouched in their chairs,
they watch the silken light fall
in a cone on the dancers,

their own legs stump branches
on blighted trunks, their arms shafts
on cranes to a scaffold.

Can the wilderness of all this
break through to their bones bleak and clamped
so tightly here in stainless steel?

Can the welded bodies will themselves
on stage, on to dancing feet
to circle, circle, circle the sound?

A dance answers itself.

2

She beckons.
He beckons.
His hand asks.
His feet ask.
She lashes forward,
Back. Yes. No.
Over, around—again again again
barely touching.
Boom—boom from the drums.
Will you? No.
No? Well, maybe.
He folds her back into a lace sandwich
as though to eat her.
Back and then. Yes.
O yes O yes O yes
and giddily, giddily
they yes yes yes yes yes off.
That's all.
Over. It's over.
Easy. So easy.

3

Down the block of mechanized chairs
only the eyes dance.
The wheels on either side are still
and the little wired bodies astride
ride no stallion to rodeo.

Why are you here? Making
me sad? It is enough
to know the deep weight
of my own body, supposedly sound,
with legs and arms that cooperate.

I am deflated after the curtain falls
never to rise with me behind it.
You punish me, cripples on wheels,
as I watch you happen into joy
for reasons unchoreographed.

In a swift reversal to prose,
the orchestra drains into its tunnel.
We sprawl to the parking lot.
Only now do the cripples whirl,
twisted hands in control of steel circles,
to sweep by us telling their story,
as in a ballet.

Eclipses

eclipse 1 —*what happened*

A scapular of birds hung fast
on the shoulders of the world
crowing and complaining
because the sun was out
behind the rindless moon.
There was darkness at quarter of two
though the world had not yet ended.
It was Saturday afternoon.
It was like the end of the world,
the sallow color of an ending
and the hush of light was like a sound.

Often back in the Garden,
another garden, a kindergarten
they had said the world was ending
when thunder hollered on East 84th Street
and the alley of street darkened
and lightning wrote its spooky script
in the sky.

The world is always ending:
day succumbs to stingy night.
Sleep travels in a pill.
Vietnam splinters in the East.
Bathwater cools, stomachs sag.
The ears harbor static.
The eye hoards cataract.
Who denies the essential flaw?
Every poem fails.

eclipse 2—*call it ecology*

It all has to do with the last going out. With death.
The salmon sinks, in its mouth the waste of centuries.
The ponderosa pine sags, its needles blunted by smog.
Tomatoes burst, gorgeous with chemicals,
as ruddypretty as the fabled apple.
Commerce tints the orange orange making it more *real*.
Mere signs of the first blight,
the initial discharge, our first going out,
the initiation into death.

In Eden the grass entangled and choked;
the fruits, the flowers, and assorted vegetables
withered after the betrayal, the fall into the state
        of death.
So it began. Who claims corruption as a cause?
It is a *memento mori*.
Death began. Acceleration is its footman.
The going down is hard.

See my father dead, his face
made puppet-live by his boyhood friend—
his body drained, tidied, plugged.
He has trickled out of himself to where he has gone.
Is it to the Eden land? O no.
The humps of rock in St. Columba's cemetery say
that stone is the final fruit of man's husbandry.

26

eclipse 3—*old men on the porch*

Done ding-donging
their limp tassels
dangle like raped bananas
inside the heart-high pants,
the flies grounded
by longing zippers
whose teeth grip each other.

They sit on the porch
in Saratoga Springs.

69   69

AL WEISS
(Palace)
Furnished Rooms • Open • Year Round

69   69

Nearby, Mother Goldsmith's
Restaurant and the Executive
Delicatessen where they never go.
Why go? They've been. Some have
wives who boil chickens, weak tea,
wives with bad feet and balding wigs.

This porch is an open coffin.
Make me know, old men, how it happens.
What takes us out when we're done?
Do you, please, sometimes meander through
that old movie, your lives, while
mumbling here in the sun?

27

eclipse 4—*a dirty poem*

Waiting for it to be noon,
then two-thirty, then five, then home.
We are waiting for supper.
We are waiting to go to bed.
We do not know that we are waiting for death.

In the Central Market an old man,
his youth in him like the lining in a pocket,
buys macaroni salad, a dill pickle,
a loaf of pudgy bread, bologna,
a coffee cake, evaporated milk.
He plots his own nutrition.
His food is an exodus,
his cravings merely scratchings on the tomb.

I hear your step
on the stairs, old man—
sig-sag, sig-sag—
your legs are creaky banisters
holding you up, getting you there.

We're all going where you already are,
and when I get there in the old-as-you-are
I too will be holding on
and humming through teeth foreign to me.
I don't care how graceful my withering,
It's one eclipse I'd gladly decline.

The going down is hard.

Which of the cottontailed microbes
will blot me up when death,
like Halley's Comet, comes speeding in
on one of his intermittent visits?

eclipse 5—*old couple at the lunch counter*

They have said everything.
Now there is only the munch
to articulate the silence.
Bite. Chew. Swallow.
Why do we live so long?
Pass the salt.
Stir the ashes.

The Death of the First Man

What was it?
How could they know what it was?
It had never happened before.
No one had ever gone out.
Whatever it was was happening.
Something was over.
Curled in a loose shape
the first dead man
drained out of himself
while the others shifted
the dead weight
(because it was dead);
they tried to make him get up.
They kicked and prodded.
Where had he gone?
Dead we now call that place
where he stayed in a heap
for maybe a week
until the stink told them
something was wrong.
Someone thought to bury him.
How could they know
from the animals that fell to their clubs
that they too could go down?
The first grave
mounded up over his weight.

What was it,
this going out?
That was what no one knew
even as it happened.
Even as it happens.

Dying

I forget
how death came.
It's a forgetting.
Death came.
I forgot how to open
my eyes.

His Necessary Darkness

From the frantic weather into his creaking tomb,
we discover the color of God.
He is the background,
the weight that surrounds him,
the thick and furry air, all bursting
in the roundness of his crescent world.
He is not the golden Man another man has made
to shimmer so that all the lightning threads should
enter into us as he on that cross
crosses over to glitter in his necessary darkness.

The whirling black, the color of God:
dense, dry like the prattle of parrots,
heady as smoke, bleak as wet furnaces to fire.
He is dangerous Coal
waiting the spastic match that can ignite
only as it grates the flint of his own dark pitch.
He is coal, dangerous and waiting.

We concede nothing
and walk as toward some banquet.
If he must, skin to skin, inform us
may we find in his conversation another spectrum,
and if he ignites, let our black ashes
celebrate his necessary darkness.

Where Have All the Nuns Gone?

1. the garb, the names

In little dresses, in brief boleros,
in mini-veils and calf-high skirts:
nurses for a Boer War. Yes.
Go away, ladies,
no longer widows of Christ
in the wonder of wide sleeves,
wider veils, hollow skirts
whipped to the wind.

What saraband will you dance
dressed for Christ's hospital
and not for his court?

Gone the garb and the names:
Mother Mary Aloysius,
Mother Sebastian of the Heart of Jesus;
Sisters St. Peter Joachim, St. Elizabeth
Thérèse, Anna Mercedes, Marie Consuela.
Gone down in legality,
back to being Bertha O'Rourkes.
Gone down with Saints Philomena, Christopher, George.

What litanies will you chant
relabeled for a saint of an aunt
and not in hosannas of sound?

2. *the language*

The L L L L L of long vigils at night,
the licorice of Latin spilling over the lips—
the language, the liquor of love.
At an alleluia the nuns rose, great Maya birds,
inside the cage of the chapel,
then rustled down to the Sanctus and bell.
In folds and hoods, the draped bodies rose,
burned and rose, as did the incense
scenting the hidden hairs in this harem of widows.

Now like the Shakers salting the earth,
hail-fellow-well-met, the nuns greet that
Great Linguist in English: 'Good
morning, God! Another fine day!'
The calisthenics of active commitment
leaving sweaty friction on the wash-and-the-wear.
How jaunty this cozy new Rotary trust
deep as a drill in the problems of mammon.
O give us this day our rye bread with crust.

3. the shape, the change

Only the minimal silhouettes now.
No two-by-two black sarcophagi
(shaped like those coffins of flesh-eating stone).
No spectacular, intricate, marvelous hats
winged and curved to fight with the wind.
No swirl of veil, no beads knocking.
An infinity of infinitives has halted all that:
to peel, to pare, to change, to decline, to go out . . .

But sometimes, sunk in an afternoon,
the ghosts come back, even the Holy Ghost,
and dance themselves dry in the old
choreography of black serge and veil.
What flaming tongues rose in *kyries*,
in *tantum*, in *ergo*, in altar-boy Latin!

What is it *to change*?
Coins in the pocket? For better, for worse?
The mind realizing that Tuesday is better?

Burial in the Sand

The sand is a gritty flesh
mounding her aching mounds.
He piles her tight
                    up to her throat.
On her head a flare of cloth hat,
in her mouth the glare of gold teeth.
Pat, pat. The drooling sand dribbles
                    over
her arthritis quiet under its warm compress.
He is Henry Moore building his old woman.
                    Then
from this burial in the sand his beach Venus
rises out of the maw of Zeus,
                    her jewelry toothy, her crown canvas.
He rises and she rises,
                    breaking the mold
the way it never happens out of
real statues, risky and rare,
although the same deep force
buried deep in the stone
is poised for the pounce.

At Jerusalem Beach on V-J Day, August 14

The surfboards scythe to an odd formation:
yellow, purple, rowdy blue pontoons carrying
    an army of one.
Sons of the warriors and some grandsons.
Jollying men jollying children seldom seen in the sun
build fortresses in the wrinkled sand.

All the wars are always on everyone's mind, somehow.
Here.
The over-populated beach is charged
with the same force, the same twitching bodies.
War.

Free from work at time-and-a-half,
The Rhode Island men spend the day armed with cigars.

The sea is weedy and the waves rise right
to where some boats once sank out of sight.
There's camouflage here in the notion that skin
is akin to skin. Legs spread in burned scissors on
    the sand.

In the Pacific, few learned to swim.
Now on this Atlantic shore they walk the floor of sand
staring, not at the sea motioning, but at each other.
The others stare back.

How in the pearly light the blood must have blanched
as it bounced in the veins on the way to Japan.
How it must have danced and made everyone
     know things
he couldn't know.

I don't know. Is this all it was for?

Man watching woman, woman the child,
charcoal smoking, meat burning, the sun turning
as the fog hiroshimas over the tangled water?

Soon to a war will the young men hasten
gliding so beautifully on sliding boards to that annex
to die or to live to this, this dying in the sun.

After the Bomb

I

Over. Morning erupts.
Light Light Light Light
dizzying pops of bulbs of dazzle.
Turner painted this city.

He knew before they did
what it was like.

His Venice trailed off
(faint cardiograph at the horizon)
next to the churning
splinters of sun, Light stems
in whirling bursts & shafts & rays & accordions
& fans of Fire Fire Fire Fire

2

The bones stick up.
Bones but not bones,
buildings in bone shapes
gnarled and arthritic shafts
once hostels to the real bones.

How quiet it is
as in cities on Sundays.

There must be something,
there must be, there must.
The grey wind carries the grey ashes
no place. There are no places.

39

Lunatic Poem

I am running from flowers . . .
I am borrowing bear . . .
It snows in the cellar.
Help me find Chapel Street . . .
Run rakes through my hair.

My mittens are talking . . .
They want me inside . . .
I'm a jar of sweet peppers.
Help me reach your conclusion.
In whose brain can I hide?

Whistle me poetry . . .
Buy me burlap . . .
Beat me, I'm dying.
Kiss me, I'm back.

Motorcycle Story

Through the crunching city
pricks the leather-bound boy in a hurry,
gaily grim and hurling flak.
The machine marries the highway.

Zing! We watch what he could not
and catch the exhaust of his words,
'O God, I am translated into blood!'

The body skips the street
like a stone on water,
but here stone on stone,
the thud of the sack he now is
mushing to the pavement.

The found sculpture of the motorcycle
drives only the forceful homily home,
the wheels whirling still, as his blood
spills to the shores of gutter
for the last wet run.

Birth Tomb

'A poem is an absence . . . The poem is an effigy.'
—Wallace Fowlie

Back in the blackness before life began
life began. The womb wore us
and we wore it. Our clothes hugged.
We were Siamese sailors floating
on and in. What a cruise!

Back in the absence before poems begin
poems begin. An urn of taut paper
filled to the edge. Words touch
in hieroglyphics branding the womb.
Birth tomb. What an effigy!

Telling It

To speak out clean.
Let the words be
not wonderful but the plainest
nouns, the skinniest verbs
that are themselves
the poem, not merely holding
it together.
The shape of poetry:
the shape of words, the words their own shapes,
the shape of many words together.
All right.
Poetry is the soup,
not the can or kettle
wrapped around it.
Telling it, telling it clean
is the meat.
Today the words are right.
They are right here.
I find what I mean
to tell myself the truth.

Poet Reading
—for Daniel Hughes

That hired suit advertised your clarity.
In black, black like a baron pirate
Or a Yeats at Stockholm for his laurels,
You stood behind the flowers and the podium
Of dream. Not in a blaze of color and delight
But hard and certain, black and white.

Once I had thought all knowledge a matter
Of margins and penmanship neat
Inside the mottled marble of those early
Copybooks. Like nuns, those black and white books
Bound truths into rigid shapes:
The feet in a mile, the square root of seven.
A poem disturbs that pattern. Knowledge cracks its
        own mold
As the line reaches out to tabulate it.

Later, when the champagne had shimmered up
Into our brains and all of our eccentricities
Were dancing, you discovered again
Beyond the dinner and the platform,
Beyond the black and white music of the host's piano,
Beyond the blond boy's rantings and his girl's dark
Tears that truth is a poet,
And in your mirror he is wearing rented clothes.

44

The Beautiful Day

If I could swallow one,
    I'd gulp down today
filling up on it.

All the wild flavor
    would summer my throat
and would fatten
    the winter's squash.

If I could kiss a day,
    I'd grab this one
and kiss it blowzy
    and plow it
for the deep thrill
    as it thrills me
being in it.

Tattoo

—for Leonard Quirino

I had forgotten
the butterfly
that lights up
your skin,
spread out in
a bright stain
of wings.

'It's my soul,' you said
and I believe it.
Now
it is obvious.
But you knew first
and had to remind me.

The soul,
a brave little carnival
right there
on your arm.

Beyond Saying

'I have nothing to say and I am saying it
and that is poetry.'
—John Cage, *Silence*

Beyond saying.
Arshile Gorki chalked
'Good-bye, my loveds' on the wall
in his suicide note.
He understood the past tense.
Everything is
beyond saying.

Touch me.
Please.

Speak
to my skin.